1

MONSTER WORLD

A Reference Guide to Some of the World's Most Scary Creatures

S. David Staggs

2

*For Rudy, Boosh, Hassan and Nick and all the long
nights sitting in dark places watching for legends.*

AGOGWE

This creature was first encountered in East Africa in 1900 by Captain William Hichens.

It's a humanoid creature said to stand between 3 and 5 feet tall with long arms and rusty colored hair. Some sightings

4

have described it as having black and gray hair.

AHOOL

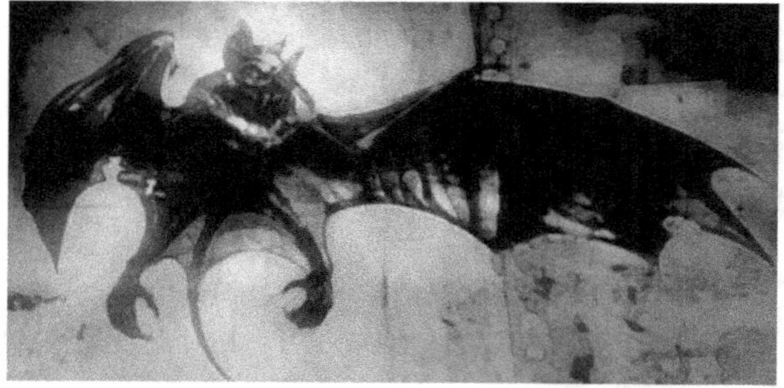

The Ahool is said to be a giant bat creature in the rain forests of Java in Indonesia. It's described as having large dark eyes, large claws, gray fur and a 10 ft wingspan. It was first described by a Dr. Ernest Bartels, who published many accounts of his explorations in the Salak Mountains.

<u>ASWANG</u>

This shapeshifting monster resides in the Philippines.
It is described as having the traits of a vampire and ghoul. It is the most feared monster in the Philippines as far back as

the 16th century.

<u>BARMANOU</u>

This bipedal primate creature is most often seen in the mountain areas of western Pakistan and Afghanistan. The sightings are reported by those that live in the mountains and describe it as being tall and hairy as well as wearing animals skins on it's backside and head.

BEAMAN

   The legend of Beaman is strong in and around Sedalia, Missouri. Although stories vary, the most common one is about a circus train that derailed in 1904. Legend says all the animals escaped and were then recovered. All but one; a 12ft

8

ape.

<u>BEAR LAKE MONSTER</u>

Bear Lake sits on the Utah/Idaho border and is said to be the home of a large beast. Descriptions vary, with some saying it resembles a serpent and has small legs to scurry along the shores. Others say it has a large body with cream colored skin and that it moved quickly through the water. The size descriptions hold it at an average of 50ft in length.

A report from 1907 states that two men claimed to see the monster attack their camp and kill one of their horses.
A four year old said to have spotted it in 1937 and a Boy Scout leader in 1946.
The last sighting was in 2002 when a local business owner claimed to see it.
The area has become a tourist attraction.

BEAST OF BLADENBORO

This mysterious monster was described as some sort of wildcat, but with an uncertain behavior and nature. It was responsible for multiple pet deaths in the winter of 1953-1954 in Bladenboro, North Carolina.

A dog was killed on the night of December 29th, 1953 by what a witness said was something "sleek, black, about 5ft long."
On December 31st, two dogs were found

dead. According to their owner, Johnny Vause, they were literally "torn into ribbons and crushed."

On January 1st, 1954, two more dogs were found dead on a local farm.

Another dog was killed sometime in the night on January 2nd, again on a local farm.

Then again, on January 3rd, another two dogs were discovered dead.

Police Chief Roy Fores spoke of an autopsy on one of the dogs. He stated, "There wasn't more than two or three drops of blood in him." He also stated that the other dogs, "The ear of one dog was gnawed off and the tongues of two had been chewed out."

During the night of January 5th, a pet rabbit was found decapitated and then on January 7th, another dog was found dead close to Bladenboro Swamp.

Many hunts were conducted for the beast but it was reported that dogs refused to follow the trails.

<u>BEAST OF BODMIN</u>

In 1978 a phantom panther type cat was said to live in and around Cornwall, England. Most of the sightings occurred in Bodmin Moor. It was also believed to be responsible for a number of livestock killings.

The Ministry of Agriculture, Fisheries and Food conducted an investigation in 1995 and found no evidence of a wildcat and suggested the livestock killings were committed by indigenous species known to the area.

<u>BEAST OF BRAY ROAD</u>

In Elkhorn, Wisconsin there sits a quiet old country road where multiple sightings have taken place of a large bipedal beast.

   The first account was reported in 1936. Sightings later boomed in the late 1980's and early 1990's. The beast has been described as sometimes bear like, sometimes hairy like Bigfoot and sometimes seen on all fours. Many accounts have it looking extremely wolf like and up to 7ft tall on two legs with it's fur described as brown and gray. The most prevalent belief is that the Beast of Bray Road is actually a werewolf.

BEAST OF BUSCO

  There is a legend in the area of Churubusco, Indiana. The legend of a massive snapping turtle that many were said to have seen in 1949. It garnered national attention when a hunt was conducted for about a month. The Beast of Busco was never found.

BEAST OF EXMOOR

In the countryside of the United Kingdom you will find Exmoor National Park. Many animals roam within but none more infamous than the Beast of Exmoor.

It's described as being a black panther in appearance. Although there were previous sightings the beast didn't get a reputation until 1983 when a farmer claimed to have lost over 100 sheep over the span of three months.

<u>BEAST OF GEVAUDAN</u>

Between 1764 and 1767, in the Margeride Mountains in the Province of Gevaudan, France, a beast terrorized the locals. It was described as a giant wolf like monster and the attacks occurred within an approximate 50 mile radius. All in all, up to 113 people were killed by the beast.

Massive hunting parties were sent out. Not only by locals but also by soldiers and royal huntsmen.

In 1765 a young girl named Marie-Jeanne Valet, was out in a small wooded area when she turned a saw the beast looking at her. When it reared up she plunged a spear into it's chest; wounding the beast but not killing it. A statue was erected in her honor later.

In 1767 the Beast of Gevaudan was shot and killed by a local hunter named Jean Chastel, ending the reign of terror.

BLACK EYED CHILDREN

Strange and disturbing encounters began
in the 1990's with what are called The
Black Eyed Children. Typically they are
seen in small groups at night and vary in
age between the approximate ages of 6
and 16. They are described as having
extremely pale skin and completely
black eyes. They are usually encountered
trying to hitch rides or showing up at the
front doors of residential homes asking
to come inside.

One such encounter took place in Texas and Brian Berthel shared his experience. As he sat in his car one night going over some paperwork, a sudden knocking hit his window. He slightly rolled down his window and looked at two boys who appeared to be around 12 years old. They kindly asked him for a ride to a nearby movie theater. Berthel then noticed their pure black eyes and felt uneasy and then frightened. He declined politely but they persisted and asked if they could get into his car. Eventually, they began to get aggressive and demanding that he let them inside (although they never tried to open the doors). Berthel finally fled away quickly.

Other encounters detail late night knocks at peoples doors. Upon opening the door, the black eyed children are found standing on their doorstep. They usually ask if they can come inside to use a phone or get warm from rain and multiple other excuses. They have never tried to rush into anyone's home, however, insisting that they be invited inside.

Those that have experienced this also describe the same feelings of fear and turn them away and shut their doors. If anyone has ever invited them inside, their stories have not surfaced.

<u>BLACK SHUCK</u>

Along the coastline and within the countryside of East Anglia in East England, wanders Black Shuck. This ghostly dog with red eyes (in some accounts green) and shaggy black hair was first encountered they say in 1577. Black Shuck is still sighted today, most often in the woods, graveyards, on roadsides and the coastline.

<u>BROSNO DRAGON</u>

In West Russia this beast is said to reside in Lake Brosno. Described as looking like a dragon, legends of the monster go back centuries. Tales of the dragon range from regular typical sightings to it flipping boats and eating fishermen.

<u>BUBAK</u>

In Slovakian folklore a horrifying creature known as the Bubak is described. It is said to look like a scarecrow and hide in the woods or near riverbanks. While hiding it emits the sound imitating a crying infant in order to lure people to it. In some tales the Bubak also has a cart that is drawn by cats.

<u>BUNYIP</u>

Said to roam rivers and lakes in Australia and described as having a dog face with tusks and dark fur. Others have described it as having a crocodile head and with flippers.

CANVEY ISLAND MONSTER

In November 1953 in England, a strange creature washed ashore on Canvey Island. The following year in August a second carcass was found on the beach.

The first body was measured at 2.4ft long and described as having a brown red skin, large gills and large eyes. It had two back legs with five digit feet but lacked any arms and appeared to be a bipedal creature.

CHANGELING

A creature from around the world believed to be some type of "fairy" or "troll." These trolls are said to take their children and switch them with human ones.

The reasoning for this varies from place to place. One reason given is that they believe their children are better off with a human upbringing. Other tales suggest they want human children to grow into slaves.

CHAMP

Lake Champlain is a long body of water that is over 100 miles long. It stretches along areas of New York and Vermont and even extends a short way into Quebec, Canada. It is within that lake that Champ, sometimes called Champy, is said to live.

 With well over 300 sightings being reported, the monster is said to be approximately 180ft long with a long neck. It's also said to have a band of red going around it's neck and a white star shape in it's forehead. Another account puts the beast at around 30ft in the length.

<u>CHUPACABRA</u>

The story of the Chupacabra begins in

Puerto Rico in March of 1995. This is when the first attack was reported. Eight sheep were found dead and completely drained of blood. It was then that it was observed that each animal had three puncture wounds on their chests.

Then, in August, around 150 animals were killed and a man claimed to see the creature.

Later, similar reports of animals killed in the same manner began to be reported

elsewhere. Places like Argentina, Chile, Peru, Brazil, Bolivia, the United States and Mexico and others.
 Based on witnesses descriptions there seems to be two separate creatures called Chupacabra.

 The first sightings described a short bipedal creature of around 4ft tall. It has dark gray or greenish skin and quills running down it's spine, large red eyes

and seen hopping.
 The other creature is described as a
strange kind of dog. Sightings have it as
mostly without hair, a large spinal ridge
and fangs and claws.

<u>DINGONEK</u>

In Africa, within the Congo jungles, is
said to live the Dingonek. It spends it's
time in rivers and lakes and is described

as being up to 19ft in length with scales, a large head with saber teeth and a scorpion tail. It's known to be territorial and said to kill anything that gets too close.

<u>DE LOYS' APE</u>

From 1917 to 1920 an expedition was led by oil geologist Francois de Loys to find petroleum around Columbia. The expedition consisted of 20 men, but due to some fighting with natives and disease, only four men came out alive.

It was while camped by the Tarra River in 1920 that they were approached by 2 large creatures. They were some type of primates and seemed angry and agitated, screaming and pointing.

Shortly after they proceeded to defecate in their hands and throw feces at the team. During this altercation one of the creatures were shot and killed. They photographed the animal.

DOBHAR-CHU

This water creature in Ireland is described as a dog and otter. It's name translates to "water hound."

The last sighting was in 2003 when Sean Corcoran and his wife saw the elusive beast. They described it as having a loud screech and orange flippers and moving extremely fast.

DOVER DEMON

While driving on April 21, 1977, seventeen year old William Bartlett said he saw a creature perched on a stone wall on Farm Street, in Dover, Massachusetts. That same night the

creature was spotted by fifteen year old John Baxter on Miller Road. Then, the following night, Abby Brabham, another fifteen year old, reported seeing a creature on Springdale Avenue.
 The creature was described as having large glowing eyes and tendril-like fingers.

<u>DYATLOV PASS INCIDENT</u>

Between February 1st and 2nd, 1959, nine

ski hikers were killed mysteriously in the Ural Mountains in Russia. The area where the deaths occurred is now known as Dyatlov Pass, named after the groups leader, Igor Dyatlov.

Sometime in the middle of the night, something happened to make them flee the safe confines of their tent without their protective clothing and gear. They fled, some even without shoes, out into heavy snowfall and subzero temperatures.

Six of the nine died due to hypothermia. The remaining three died from physical trauma. Two suffered major chest fractures and the other a fractured skull. One was also missing their tongue.

Investigators concluded the injuries were not caused by people, stating the injuries were bad enough to have been caused by a severe automobile accident.

 The tent had been cut open from the inside while in a panic before they ran into the elements. What could have caused them to run out unprotected in -30 temperature?

 The cause of death was ruled as being caused by an "unknown compelling force."

 It remains a mystery to this day.

<u>ENFIELD MONSTER</u>

 In April of 1973, reports began coming in around Enfield, Illinois. It began on April 25th, at about 9:30pm, when a man named Henry McDaniel heard a scratching sound at his door. He grabbed his gun and flashlight to go outside and investigate.

  Upon looking around he spotted a creature standing between two rose bushes. He went on to describe it later, stating "It had three legs on it, a short body, two little short arms and two pink eyes as big as flashlights. It stood four and a half feet tall and was grayish-colored."

FLATWOODS MONSTER

Also known as the Phantom of
Flatwoods, this mysterious creature was
sighted in Flatwoods, West Virginia, on

September 12, 1952.

The majority of the witnesses described it as around 7ft tall. It's body and face were said to be black and dark in color and had a glowing face. A large and tall cowl was said to be behind it's head.

FOUKE MONSTER

Between 1971 and 1974, around Fouke, Arkansas, many encountered a large beast deemed by many to be a Sasquatch. It was also known as the Southern Sasquatch and Beast of Boggy Creek. This creature through various witnesses put it at between 7 and 10ft in height with an estimated weight of between 300 and 800 pounds.

 Reports also describe it as having long dark hair and having a horrible smell, like a wet dog and skunk. Some tracks were found and they appeared to show that the creature had three toes. This is one of the only pieces of evidence that differs from Sasquatch reports, as those prints have five toes.

On the night of May 2, 1971, the Fouke Monster reportedly attacked the home of Bobby Ford and his wife Elizabeth. The creature reached it's arm through an open window as Elizabeth slept on the couch. Her husband and brother-in-law took shots at the beast and thought that they hit it as it fled into the dark woods. No blood was later found, however, there were claw marks on the porch and nearby they discovered three-toed tracks.

The reports rolled in after that. The last reported sightings were in 2010.

GHOUL

A ghoul is said to be a particularly grotesque creature that dwells within graveyards and other burial grounds. The skinny undead looking monster is said to feed on the flesh of the dead and is nocturnal. It's also believed that they set small fires in desolate areas to try and lure travelers in.

<u>GNOME</u>

A Gnome is described as a very small, short creature with a pointy hat. They are mischievous and perhaps even evil. Although it may sound humorous, there have actually been many frightening reports of Gnomes from around the world.

Like the Gnome or Gnomes that terrorized a woman named Tammy Thomas and her children at a farm house in Porterville, California. A former resident of the home also said to have encountered the creatures on the property.

 Then, on March 11, 2008, at around 1:00am near a small town in Argentina, a Gnome was spotted by a group of teens. They heard some rustling in a highly overgrown area a short distance away. They then captured on a phone camera a small creature with a pointy hat (above) do a sideways shuffle out onto the road. The video abruptly stops soon after as the teens flee.

<u>GOATMAN</u>

An urban legend runs strong in Beltsville, Maryland. It's here where the infamous Goatman is said to stalk around back roads late at night. He is described as half man and half goat that carries an axe. It's even said that he has attacked several cars with this axe.

The most sightings are said to happen on Fletchertown Road, where it's claimed he attacks the cars of people parked at a local Lover's Lane.

<u>HELLHOUND</u>

These phantom black dogs with glowing red eyes have been reported worldwide, with many of the sightings occurring in graveyards.

They are believed by some to be guards of secrecy, trying to keep some supernatural creatures hidden. In other stories they are said to be hunters of lost souls.

IGOPOGO

 Lurking in Lake Simcoe in Ontario, Canada, is a mystery creature known as the Igopogo. It's described as a long creature with a canine type head. Some witnesses even claim they've seen it on the shores.

<u>INDRID COLD</u>

 Also known as the "grinning man" he is said to look completely human, but it's the consensus of most that he is not. At least not completely. He's described as having a darker complexion and over 6ft in height. Other accounts also state he has no hair, nose or ears. When first encountered he was wearing a shiny reflective green suit. A later account said he wore a blue one.

The first encounter happened in New Jersey on October 16, 1966. Two boys spotted him standing near a fence. The man in the green metal looking suit was grinning at them and then proceeded to chase the boys until they lost him. It should be noted that there were also multiple UFO sightings reported in the area around this time and many believe Indrid Cold to be an extraterrestrial or human hybrid.

He was encountered again two more times in West Virginia at the same time the Mothman incidents were occuring, which also saw multiple UFO sightings.

JERSEY DEVIL

  Described as having a goat type head, claws and bat like wings, the infamous Jersey Devil is said to dwell within the Pine Barrens of New Jersey. Other accounts also say it has cloven feet and a chilling scream heard on many late nights.

  Many encounters have been reported,

even one by a credible police officer. Sightings range from seeing it fly over or coming face to face with the 12ft monster in the Pine Barrens.

KRAKEN

Said to inhabit the seas off of the coast on Norway and Greenland, this massive beast is said to be up to 50ft in length.

It's believed to be a massive octopus or giant squid.

<u>LAKE WORTH MONSTER</u>

 The Monster of Lake Worth, near Fort Worth, Texas, is described as being what appears to be half goat and half man with scales and fur. Multiple reports flooded in, including one in 1969 when a man claimed the monster jumped down from a tree and landed on his car.

LOCH NESS MONSTER

The notorious Loch Ness Monster is a massive creature said to live in Loch Ness in Scotland. It's described as having a long neck and large head it occasionally raises out of the water and four large flippers. Initial reports began in 1933 and many sightings are still reported today.

<u>LOVELAND FROG</u>

This bizarre creature was first spotted in 1955. As the story goes, a traveling salesman saw three of these amphibian looking bipedal animals near a river or on a bridge.

Then in 1972 on March 3rd, at approximately 1:00am, police officer Ray Shockley spotted one of these creatures. He was driving down Riverside Drive when the thing scurried across the road. He described it as 3-4ft tall and was standing upright. He said it looked right at him before hopping over a guardrail and vanishing into the river.

A couple weeks later, Officer Mark Matthews claimed to sight the creature and even shoot at it, however, he later recanted his statement on the incident.

<u>MANANANGGAL</u>

Said to attack and feed on sleeping people in the Philippines, this monster is one of the most horrid creatures said to reside here. The monster is a vampire type monster but has the ability to detach it's upper torso from the rest of it's body. It then flies away with bat like wings to seek out sleeping people to feed upon.

During the splitting of it's body is when it is said to be the most vulnerable. Local legend states that if the lower half of the body is found, then putting salt, garlic and or ash on it will destroy the creature. The monster will no longer be able to attach it's self back and die when the sun rises.

MAN-EATING TREE

THE YA-TE-VEO, OR CARNIVOROUS PLANT. 476

In a few parts of the world are said to be large carnivorous plants capable of devouring a human being. One example is the Madagascar Tree. A well known report claimed that the Mkodo tribe of Madagascar sacrificed someone to this tree, whose vine's quickly wrapped them up and constricted them.

Two other plants were supposedly discovered in Central America. The Vampire Vine, said to latch on and drain the blood of anything it grabs, and the Ya-Te-Veo, with serpent like vines that strike out.

<u>MAPINGUARI</u>

Deep within the Amazon it is said that a beast known as the Mapinguari roams about.

   This creature has been described as being roughly 7ft tall and covered with red hair over a thick hide. It has long arms with large claws and appears very sloth like in appearance. However, it's most interesting description, is that it is said to have one eye and a second, larger mouth on it's stomach.

Locals say it has a putrid smell and although aggressive, it is slow. Of course, that presents a danger within itself, being able to move very quietly. It's also believed to be a carnivore and was blamed in 1937 for killing over 100 cows and ripping their tongues out over a three week period.

MELON HEADS

These small humanoid creatures with

enlarged heads are said to hide in dark areas and are known to attack people occasionally. They've been spotted in wooded areas and on dark back roads. They are mostly sighted in parts of Ohio, Michigan and Connecticut.

<u>MERMAIDS</u>

Everyone knows the famed descriptions of Mermaids and Mermen as having the upper body of something humanoid in appearance and the lower half a fish like body with a tail.

In many cases, Mermaids have been known as kind creatures, while other accounts have them luring people to their deaths. Mermaid sightings continue to this day and some interesting and compelling evidence has also been gathered.

MICHIGAN DOGMAN

The first encounter with this werewolf type monster occurred when a couple of lumberjacks saw the creature in 1887. Being described as a wolf with a mans body, it was also encountered in 1937, the 1950's and in 1967.

MOMO

With hair said to resemble a shag rug carpet, the possible Sasquatch known as Momo dwells in Missouri. Also described as being 7ft tall with black hair and emitting a foul odor.
 Momo was spotted many times over the summer of 1972.

<u>MONGOLIAN DEATH WORM</u>

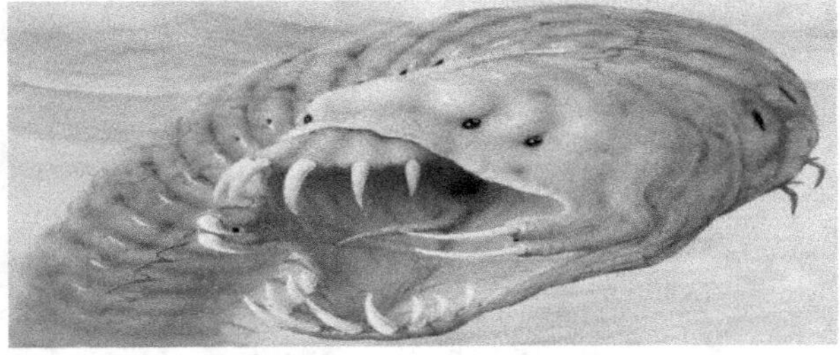

This fearsome worm dwells in the sands of the Gobi Desert, where it remains mostly dormant aside from June and July. The Mongolian people believe touching the creature can cause death. It's said to spit an acidic venom at people, as well as cause electric shocks. Another belief is that they kill camels and lay their eggs within their intestines.

MONKEY-MAN OF DELHI

In New Delhi, India, reports began to flood in about a creature in May, 2001. This four foot tall monkey type creature kept appearing each night and even attacked people. Many sustained injuries and there were also a few deaths as a result of panic, when some jumped from rooftops or fell down stairs trying to get away from the little monster. Fifteen people suffered scratches and bites on the night of May 13th alone. The creature seen jumping rooftops was described as having black hair, long claws, red eyes and wearing a helmet of some sort.

MONTAUK MONSTER

In Montauk, New York, four young friends stumbled upon the corpse of an unidentified creature on July 12, 2008.

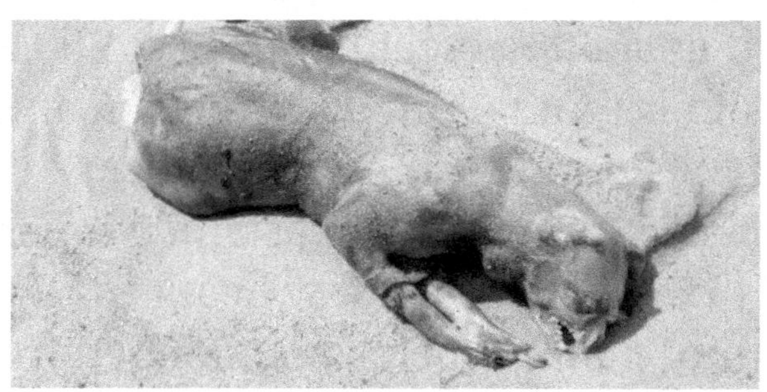

The carcass found at the Ditch Plains Beach is said to have mysteriously vanished and speculations about the strange animal continue.

MOTHMAN

This terrifying monster terrorized areas around Point Pleasant, West Virginia, from November 12, 1966 to December 15, 1967. It is described as humanoid, but dark with glowing red eyes and having huge wings.

One particular night, November 15, 1966, two young couples, Roger Scarberry and his wife, Linda, along with Steve and Mary Mallette, encountered the Mothman outside of town in the area known as the "TNT Area." During World War II it was the site of a munitions plant.

Sighting reports began to come in from all over the area, until on December 15, 1967, when the nearby Silver Bridge collapsed, resulting in the death of 46 people.

Sightings stopped for awhile and some believe there was a connection between the collapse and the Mothman.

Today there is an annual Mothman Festival and a 12ft tall statue of the creature sits in the middle of town.

OGOPOGO

 Okanagan Lake, in British Columbia, Canada, is the home of a sea serpent looking beast known as the Ogopogo. Witness accounts suggest it to be between 40-50ft long. The creature has had sightings from 1926 to 2011.

<u>OLD YELLOW TOP</u>

 This Sasquatch type beast of a said 7ft height was reported multiple times around Cobalt, Ontario, Canada. Witnesses described what appears to be a Sasquatch but has blonde hair on it's head, hence the nickname. The sightings date back to 1906 with the last sighting occurring in 1970.

<u>OLITIAU</u>

Said to be a giant bat that dwells in Central America. It was encountered by a couple of hunters in 1932 that said it swooped down at them. They described it as having a wingspan of 6-12ft, black, and having two inch serrated teeth.

ORANG-BATI

Tales of this beast date back to the 15th

century. It's described as an incredibly large monkey type creature with bat like wings that attacks villages on the Island of Seram in Indonesia.

<u>ORANG PENDEK</u>

In the mountain forests of Sumatra, many have claimed to have encountered a monster they call Orang Pendek. Tribes and villagers have been documenting run ins with the beast for about 100 years. It's described as around 5ft tall, covered in dark brown or orange fur and primate in nature.

<u>OWLMAN</u>

This strange creature was seen in the village of Mawnan, Cornwall, England in 1976. The Owlman was first reported by two young girls who described it as looking like a man with feathers and wings.

OZARK HOWLER

Described as being the size of a bear with shaggy black hair and having horns. The Howler roams dark countrysides in Arkansas, Missouri and Texas. It's howls and cries in the night are said to sound like a blend of a wolf and an elk's bugle.

<u>POPOBAWA</u>

Zanzibar, Tanzania is said to be the home of an incredibly feared monster known as the Popobawa. Its most common description is being a lean, tall, bipedal bat like creature with one large eye. However, it is also believed to be a shapeshifter that can take human and animal forms, the bat creature being it's true form.

In 1995, after multiple sightings, a mass panic gripped the region. Every time sightings are reported, panics set in, generally in Zanzibar. During these panics, people, families and neighbors stay close together outside around a fire all night.

<u>PUKWUDGIE</u>

  These 3ft creatures are said to reside in Delaware. The troll like creatures are said to be intelligent and reclusive, as well as aggressive. Native Americans believe there was a time when they were overall friendly to humans, but later turned against them for unknown reasons.

  Some legends say they can appear suddenly and then vanish. They're said to use arrows and spears and attack with small knives. They are as well known to push people off of cliffs.

<u>SASQUATCH</u>

The most well known monster in the United States and other parts of the world is the Sasquatch. More commonly known as "Bigfoot."

Described as between 7 and 9ft tall, these humanoid hairy beasts are known to roam wooded areas nationwide with sightings reported in every state. Over the decades, thousands upon thousands of sightings and encounters have been documented. Enough gathered to really form a behavioral profile of the creatures.

Washington state has the most reported sightings and a huge amount are reported in the Pacific Northwest. However, there's many hot spots in the east as well, like Salt Fork State Park and the Cuyahoga Valley National Park, both located in Ohio.

Evidence is constantly gathered, from footprints to photographs and footage. One of the most compelling pieces of evidence is the famous Patterson-Gimlin footage. The 59 second film was shot by Roger Patterson and Robert Gimlin at Bluff Creek in northern California in 1967. The video shows a tall, large primate looking creature walking fully upright into the woods and even looking back at them.

Although many have tried to claim the footage a hoax, one can clearly see muscle movement under the skin and fur. The footage has been analyzed by experts for years and one movie studio spent thousands of dollars to recreate the footage with practical effects and failed to make it even look close.

Based on the majority of the reports the creatures are timid and like to be left alone. However, they are also territorial and defensive, with some throwing rocks and chasing people away.

Some witnesses have reported sounds of

whispering or soft talking yet can't make out any words. This has led many to believe that they have their own pseudolanguage.

 Another thing they are known for is building strange dome like structures with sticks and vines as well as set up weird stick formations. Some believe they are a form of communication to others. Another key report is their screams in the night, a loud guttural scream a few times in a row. Other times a "whooping" sound, also a few times in a row, as well as a low, long howling.
 Lastly, they're known for "tree knocks." This is where they take a branch or stick and hit it against a tree, again multiple times. The knocks are often heard deep in the woods at night in hot spots or where sightings have been.

<u>SKINWALKERS</u>

These witches and warlocks in Navajo legend are believed to be able to take animal form, primarily a wolf like creature. Skinwalkers are shunned by their people but their identity isn't typically known. Legend says if you call a Skinwalker by his or hers true human name, it will kill it.

 Many people have reported having terrifying encounters with Skinwalkers, with some being witnessed outside of people's homes or looking in windows. Other common sightings are of them running along the side of cars and looking at you through the window. A police officer once reported a similar encounter.

 Skinwalkers are most often seen out west in places like Utah, New Mexico, Nevada and Arizona.

<u>SNALLYGASTER</u>

Legends of this monster were started in the 1730's by German immigrants that settled around the hills of Washington D.C. And Maryland. It's described as having massive wings, hook like claws, one eye and a large beak full of teeth. Other accounts claim it also has tentacles. It would swoop down and grab people and carry them off to devour.

SPRING-HEELED JACK

This strange odd creature was first encountered in 1837. He was described by witnesses as having claws and eyes that they said resembled "red balls of fire."

His claws were said to be metallic and he wore a black cloak and some kind of helmet. Multiple separate reports claimed he could also breathe blue and white fire and that he is lean and tall.

He was known to make great leaps and jumps over walls and across rooftops all over London while terrorizing people and clawing some. The last reported sighting was in Liverpool in 1904.

<u>THUNDERBIRD</u>

Thunderbird stories date back hundreds of years in Native American culture. This giant bird is believed to have a wingspan up to 18ft. Sightings and reports go back to the 1800's. More occurred in the 1940's and 1970's. Reports have come in from different parts of the country. More recent sightings are one in 2002 when a large bird was spotted with a 14ft wingspan in Alaska and sightings were also documented in 2007 near San Antonio, Texas.

<u>VAMPIRES</u>

These creatures of the night are known in every part of the world. Undead corpses that rise each night to feed on the blood of the living.

Many cultures vary in belief of what a vampire truly is. Some believe it to be some kind of sickness and can be transferred to others via bites. Others believe they are demonically possessed corpses and some believe them to be actually alive and not undead at all. In some nations, cages were placed over the graves of people suspected to be vampires in order to keep them contained each night.

There are many historical cases that give credence to the existence of vampires.

THE VAMPIRE OF CROGLIN GRANGE

This story is generally regarded as folklore, but the tale bares mentioning. It begins in 1875 when a country home in Cumberland, England, was rented to two brothers, Edward and Michael Cranswell and their sister, Amelia Cranswell.

 One night a creature came through Amelia's window and attacked her; biting her throat. Her screams brought her brothers running into the room and the vampire was gone. As one brother tended to his sister, the other pursued the monster, but to no avail.

 The following year the creature returned again, but this time one of the brothers managed to shoot it in the leg. They were able to track it down to a crypt in a graveyard, but opted to wait until day to enter. After the sun rose they went into the vault and found a creature sleeping inside a coffin with a gunshot wound to it's leg. They burned the vampire and the coffin and left.

ARNOLD PAOLE

This case took place in the village of Meduegna, near the west Morava River in Trstenik, Serbia. Arnold Paole died in or around 1725 after falling from a hay wagon and breaking his neck. At one time, before returning to his village, he had claimed to be attacked by a vampire in an area around modern day Kosovo. He said he had cured the infliction by smearing himself in blood and devouring dirt from the monsters grave.

About a month after his demise, four villagers claimed Paole visited them and plagued them at night. Shortly after all four fell ill and died. Recalling his tales of his encounters with a vampire, villagers opened Paole's grave 10 days later.

His corpse was not decomposed at all and he had blood on his face, mouth, shirt and all around inside his coffin. His fingers and toe nails were off and new ones had grown and layers of skin appeared shed. The official report continues to say that a wooden stake was driven through his heart, and those present said he shrieked and groaned and bled. His body was beheaded and his remains burned.

Afterwards, they dug up his four presumed victims and did the same to them.

Five years later, some newcomers to the village within the past six months were thought to cause a second outbreak. 13 people died of sudden illness in a 6 week period. Two women, Milica and Stana, claimed to have had vampiric encounters. 17 people ended up dying. One of them had claimed one of the dead had entered her room in the night and attacked her. Days later she was dead as well. Again, they were all dug up and given the same treatment as Paole and his victims. These deaths were also attributed to Paole after it was said he had also killed several oxen that the villagers ate.

PETER PLOGOJOWITZ

Peter Plogojowitz died in 1725 in the village of Kisilova, Serbia. Within 8 days after his death, 9 other villagers died as well. Each one, before their death, said that Plogojowitz attacked them in the night. His wife even claimed that after his death he walked in one night looking for his shoes. She quickly moved to another village.

Le Vampire, lithographie de R. de Moraine, tirée des *Tribunaux secrets*.

Plogojowitz was exhumed and found in the same conditions as Arnold Paole. He was staked and burned.

THE HIGHGATE VAMPIRE

Publicity about the Highgate Vampire began in December, 1969 when a young man named David Farrant spent a night within the cemetery. He reported a gray figure and his friends also claimed to hear and see things inside, although none of them described the same things.

Another man, Sean Manchester, also believed something was residing inside the gates. He believed it was a vampire. To be exact, an unknown nobleman from medieval Romania. He went on to say that the vampire was brought there in it's coffin by human caretakers in the early 1800's and that they bought him a house somewhere in the West End. He then stated the monster was buried in what later became Hightgate Cemetery.

Soon, a rivalry emerged between Manchester and Farrant, both determined to destroy the creature. Manchester announced a public hunt on March 13, 1970. Mobs of people flooded into the locked cemetery against police orders. No creature was found.

Years later, Manchester and some others entered the cemetery late one night to investigate a crypt a psychic had told him about. They were unable to open the door but got inside via a hole in the roof. Once inside, they found a number of empty coffins and proceeded to sprinkle holy water and place garlic.

On August 1, 1970, a headless body was discovered near the crypt. That remained a mystery. Farrant was arrested some time later after being caught inside the cemetery. However, the case was later dismissed.

Days after his arrest, Manchester and his crew returned to the cemetery during the day and went to a different crypt instructed to them from the psychic. With much effort they finally managed to get inside. Once inside, Manchester opened a coffin to find a corpse that was not decomposed. He was about to drive a stake into it when a companion stopped him and urged him against it. He hesitated but then closed the coffin and put garlic within the tomb as well as incense.

Manchester claimed to return three years later and discovered this same vampire sleeping in the cellar of an empty house. This time he said he staked and burned the creature. Upon staking it, he said it let out a groan and began to decay rapidly until it was mostly skeletal. He provided photographs of this.

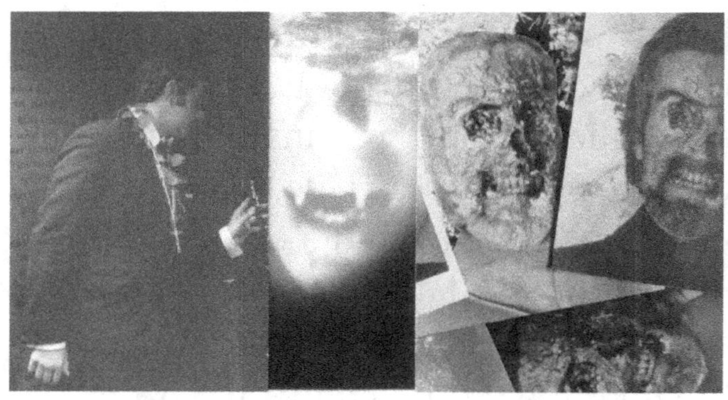

The debate of the Highgate Vampire continues today. As does the feud between Manchester and Farrant.

WENDIGO

In the Great Lakes region of the United States and Canada and northern woodlands of the east coast, is said to live horrible monsters known as Wendigo's.

They are said to be more active in the winter months and are associated with cannibalism. It is believed that a cannibal could turn into one of these creatures and that some of them were in fact once human. Another belief is that someone could become a Wendigo by being around them for a prolonged period.

They are described as extremely lean with tight skin over their bones and being gray in color. Some say they are also very tall and have antlers.

WEREWOLVES

The belief in werewolves, sometimes called Lycanthrope's, dates back as far as 1100. These beasts are human and have the ability to shapeshift into a large wolf like creature. It's a common belief that werewolves turn based on the full moon., typically the night before, night of, and night after. Other's, however, don't believe they have anything to do with the lunar cycle and chalk that up to folklore, just as some do with the silver bullet belief.

To lend credence to this, some who believe creatures such as the Beast of Bray Road are werewolves will point out that the sightings did not occur on nights of a full moon. Meanwhile, sightings of some other werewolf type creatures did in fact occur during a full moon.

Another long held belief is that while in their wolf form they are purely animal with no control or recollection. Other's believe they retain themselves and their human intellect while turned. Anyone's guess to any of these questions are as good as anyone else's.

 To become a werewolf, the two most known ways are to be bitten by one or drink rain water from a werewolf's paw print. As for weaknesses, silver and the poisonous flower wolfsbane are said to be fatal to them.
 Many werewolf encounters have been documented all over the world and across the United States.

<u>YEREN</u>

Known as China's Bigfoot, the Yeren is said to live in the mountains of China. It's described as having reddish brown hair and reports generally have it at around 8ft tall, but some have said about 12ft. Other accounts have it having all white hair as well.

YETI

 This elusive monster resides in the Himalayan Mountains in Nepal, Tibet. Also known as the Abominable Snowman, is said to be around 8ft tall and covered in white hair.

 Sightings began in the 1800's and have

persisted. Tracks were photographed in 1951 by a man named Eric Shipton. Josh Gates and his team from *SyFy's Destination Truth* discovered tracks there in 2007 and molds were taken. He returned in 2009 to investigate further and obtained a hair sample. Forensic analysis discovered an unknown DNA sequence.

<u>YOWIE</u>

The Yowie is a large bipedal creature that resides in Australia. It's described as between 6 and 12ft tall and covered in hair like a Sasquatch. However, the prints found differ and the Yowie has been described as highly aggressive and violent. Sightings and encounters have been reported since the 1800's and continue today.

<u>ZOMBIES</u>

  Typically viewed as a reanimated corpse that attacks and feeds on the living. Zombies actually date back to slaves in Haiti. People were poisoned and appeared dead and thus were buried. Later, the one responsible would dig them up and they would be in a mindless "zombie like" state. From here they were used as work slaves. Many reports surfaced in the 1900's of dead people seen years later wandering the streets aimlessly.

  Down the road the term evolved and zombies are more often seen as undead monsters reanimated by a pathogen or other means.

__CLOSING__

As I did in the companion book, Ghost World, I wanted to give a little advice from experience. Ghosts and spirits have their dangers and risks as I pointed out, but now we're talking about physical creatures/animals which present a danger that needs not be detailed. For amateur cryptozoologists it should go without saying to use your head, by all means don't go looking to provoke a Sasquatch or other beast. Go in with caution and make sure all your bases are covered. Specifically, knowledge of a creature you're looking for and equipment for the environments you'll be trekking.

Be safe and happy hunting.
-S

114